The Falkland Islands

Between the Wind & Sea

King Penguins do not bother building a nest, but incubate their eggs on top of their feet beneath a flap of warm, bare skin. *Volunteer Point.*

The Falkland Islands

Between the Wind & Sea

Kevin Schafer

COACH HOUSE PUBLICATIONS

ISLE OF WIGHT

ENGLAND

Front Cover Photograph, Adult and baby Black-browed Albatross, New Island.

ISBN: 1-899-392-262

COACH HOUSE PUBLICATIONS LIMITED

ISLE OF WIGHT, ENGLAND

The Coach House, School Green Road, Freshwater, Isle of Wight, PO40 9BB
Tel: +44 (0) 1983 755 655

Further copies of this book can be obtained from the publishers by contacting us at the address above
or via our online ordering service at www.coachhouseonline.co.uk

Printed in the UK by LPC Printing Ltd
Book Design by David Bowles

Table OF Contents

A Gentoo Penguin, just home from the sea, prepares to feed its young chicks on Saunders Island.

Foreword

It has been said that more people cross the Brooklyn Bridge everyday into Manhattan than have ever visited the Falkland Islands. For those of you who haven't yet made this trip, let me try to persuade you why you should.

This fragmented archipelago with thousands of miles of rugged and natural coastlines contains two-thirds of the world's breeding Black-browed Albatross. In reality that means that this is the most accessible place on the planet where you can lie on a cliff-top, listening to the sea crash and watch these incredible birds swoop above you as they return to their nests. In the same day you can see one of the world's rarest birds of prey, the inquisitive and incredibly tame Striated Caracara, watch sea lions and elephant seals sunbathing in the shelter of Tussac Grass and study dolphins as they play in the shallows. In short, the Falklands is untouched wild beauty at its finest.

However, threats to the wildlife abound here and have done since the early days of sealers and whalers. Our seabirds are desperately in need of protection. Fishing poses a grave danger of both competition and by-catch and two Black-browed Albatross per hour die on long-lines and the warp lines of trawlers. Unexplained penguin deaths may mirror some larger scale global change that bodes ill for these birds. Oil and mineral exploration is a real threat in the future and on land, agricultural practice and pasture improvement programmes threaten the native flora. Tourism has undergone a five-fold increase in the last five years, without any of the protection present in other parts of the world.

Visitors, however, could also be our saving grace. The Falklands is not an open-air zoo, with fences and signs. It retains the wide horizons and open vistas that attract the free of spirit and it is this essence that all with a love of nature and its bounties should strive to protect. I hope that after reading this book you will feel the same.

Becky Ingham
Falklands Conservation
Stanley, October 2003

Late afternoon light bathes a Black-browed Albatross colony at the north end of New Island. The offshore islands are among the most magical places in the Falklands, where wind and surf and stone – and life itself – seem to merge.

Introduction & Acknowledgements

During the early 1980's, I stumbled onto a well-worn copy of a book by American ornithologist Olin Sewall Pettingill, describing his research on seabirds in the South Atlantic. The book was "Another Penguin Summer", and it was a revelation, filled with pictures of penguin-covered beaches and raw, wild scenery in a place I had never heard of : The Falkland Islands. As a young photographer, mad about both seabirds and islands, it looked like nothing short of paradise. Today, twenty years later, it still does.

It is never easy to explain the nature of obsession or enchantment, but somehow these far-flung islands have lodged themselves firmly in my soul. Perhaps it is simply because they have given me the rare opportunity to immerse myself completely in the world of wildlife, alone and unfettered, in a way that is impossible almost anywhere else in the world. On our first trip to the Falklands, my wife Marty and I spent a full month in the islands, with no agenda other than to spend as much time as possible in the company of animals. For me, they were days of delirious, windswept joy. In a word: heaven. Since then, I have made two more journeys south, always during the brief, whirlwind months of the austral summer when wildlife activity is at its peak. (Someday I hope to return in the winter, if only to savour the sharp, brilliant light.) When I am in the Falklands, life becomes almost monastic, with long days of quiet wandering along cliff-top and moorland. The camera is often just an afterthought: I spend most of my time sitting, and watching, oblivious to the weather.

This book, then, is a record of those three extended stays in the Falklands, a collection of pictures and stories from a place I hold dear. It is, inevitably, incomplete: I have not given every island equal time, nor did I set out to record every bird or flower. Fortunately, there are other, more scholarly books available for the serious naturalist - chief among them several excellent books by Ian Strange (see the bibliography). My contribution, by contrast, is more visual than scientific, more celebration than field guide. Whatever it is, this book would never have materialized at all had it not been for the generous help, and fine company, of many good friends in the Falklands. Chief among these are Kim and Tony Chater of New Island North, warm hosts and fine company, who opened their magical island to us, kindly offering us the splendours of the Virgin Hotel, along with great rashers of fresh lamb. I am grateful as well to Allan White and Jacqui Jennings, both native Falklanders who have been invariably gracious and kind towards this enthusiastic outsider. I also want to thank David and Suzan Pole-Evans, of Saunders Island, especially for their dedication in preserving the wildlife at the Neck - one of the most glorious places in the islands. Rod and Lily Napier were kind enough to let us spend several unforgettable days on West Point Island: a wild, wonderful place. Similarly, Rob McGill hosted us several times on tranquil Carcass Island, and insisted on feeding us to within an inch of our lives.

Special thanks go to Tony Hall, of Coach House Publications, for taking on this book project with such enthusiasm, and for staying the course. Tony gave up his room in Stanley for us once, a generous act that, quite unexpectedly, resulted in this book. For both the book - and the bed - I am grateful.

And finally, a very special word of thanks to everyone at Falklands Conservation in Stanley, especially to Becky Ingham, Andrea Clausen, and Nic Huin. Charged with monitoring the changes and challenges that confront the natural environment of the Falklands, they are dedicated people doing important work on all our behalf. Simply said, there is something heroic in their caring stewardship of these splendid islands and we are all in their debt.

CHAPTER ONE

The Far Edge of the World

On the first day of March,1833, a 27-meter bark-rigged sailing ship dropped anchor in the shallow harbour of Port Louis in the Falkland Islands. The ship was the "HMS Beagle", and aboard was twenty-four year-old naturalist Charles Darwin, in the middle of the legendary voyage that would carry him into history.

Darwin spent several weeks in the Falklands, exploring the islands on horseback, and recording his observations on the islands' natural history. He was not, by all accounts, charmed by the place. Writing in his journal, later published as "The Voyage of the Beagle," he refers to the Falklands simply as "these miserable islands, ...desolate and wretched... of a monotonous brown colour."

To be fair, it appears to have rained most of the time. Yet Darwin's rather grim appraisal of the Falklands has always struck me as decidedly uncharitable. Yes, these islands could be accused of a slight over-abundance of weather, but they can also be wild, dramatic - and exquisitely beautiful. And where the land meets the sea, one of the richest corners of the ocean, the islands can suddenly explode with life. In places, the gatherings of wildlife in the Falkland Islands rival anything on the planet.

A sublimely beautiful day on New Island, where lichen-covered slabs of rock outline a small colony of Black-browed Albatross. In the distance are North and Saddle Islands, important wildlife refuges.

Watching penguins coming ashore through the surf, or elephant seals wallowing in the sand, it may be difficult to remember that the Falklands lie at exactly the same relative latitude as London. Yet instead of the balmy Gulf Stream that warms British shores, the Falklands are bathed by colder stuff - remnants of the Southern Ocean current that encircles Antarctica.

The result is a climate that, while typically cool, is surprisingly mild. Yet it is not temperature that defines these islands, but wind. Steady, persistent winds make the weather in the Falklands seem unnaturally restless: even in mid-summer the skies can turn dark and disagreeable, with stinging rain. Then, just as quickly, the clouds can part and the islands suddenly sparkle in the bright southern air. (What Sean Connery once said of Edinburgh holds true here: there is no such thing as bad weather, just incorrect clothing.)

The Falklands stretch 250 kilometres from east to west, and total some 12,200 square kilometres of land. With as many as four hundred islands, large and small, the Falkland coastline is endlessly varied, with gentle, lapping shorelines, and towering cliffs, pounded by the surf. By contrast, most of the interior of the islands is more bucolic, with vast expanses of open moorland divided by gentle ranges of smooth, broad-shouldered quartzite hills.

The highest peak in the Falklands is Mt. Usborne, a modest rise on Wickham Heights, the long chain of hills that forms the rocky spine of East Falkland. At only 705 meters, Usborne is no giant, yet high enough to have gathered glaciers on its flanks during the Ice Age, as evidenced by its sheer northern headwalls and cluster of blue-black tarns.

Like feathered missiles, these Gentoos burst out of the breaking surf on a New Island beach as if in a hurry to get ashore. Perhaps they are - sea lions regularly patrol this beach and take any penguins they can catch.

On Sea Lion Island, the setting sun casts long shadows from thousands of roosting Imperial Cormorants. Nearby is the memorial for the HMS Sheffield, the Royal Navy destroyer that was sunk on May 4, 1982, with the loss of 21 men.

Another legacy of the Pleistocene ice is what many consider the Falklands' most striking physical feature: her "Stone Runs." Like petrified rivers, frozen in time, stone runs drape many of the higher slopes and upland valleys, especially on East Falkland.

From the air, they appear almost liquid, flowing gracefully from the highlands toward the sea. At ground level, however, their grace vanishes in chaotic heaps of stone: crossing one on foot is an ankle-breaking horror.

Although scientists have long puzzled over the origin of these great "streams of stones," as Darwin called them, most now agree that they are relics of the sharp freeze-thaw cycles that accompanied the islands' repeated glacial periods. Water collecting in cracks in the rock during the day froze at night, expanding with enough power to split great boulders in half. These splintered rocks were then carried down-slope by the combined efforts of gravity and the slow creep of saturated soil underneath. The process would likely have been imperceptibly slow, and the stone runs taken thousands of years to form.

Geologically, the Falklands are an anomaly. For despite their proximity to the Patagonian mainland, these islands are composed of rocks with affinities far to the east – in what is today Southern Africa. The Falklands are, in fact, wayward chips of ancient Gondwanaland, that great super-continent that began to split apart two hundred million years ago. Broken off the African coast, they were set adrift across the widening Atlantic where they would, fifty million years later, fetch up hard on the edge of the New World.

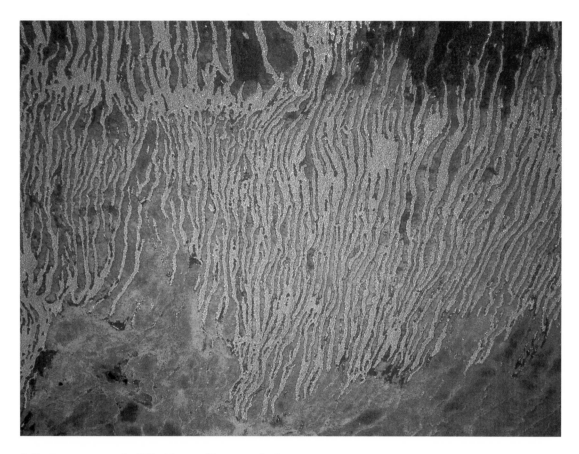

As if molten, stone runs on East Falkland form a striking pattern of rock and vegetation from the air. No wonder that this phenomenon has fascinated and puzzled visitors since Darwin's day.

A variety of lichens decorate the exposed layers of rock at Seal Bay, along the remote northern coast of East Falkland. It would take a lifetime – albeit a happy one - to explore the thousands of miles of shorelines in this wild archipelago.

A Giant Petrel – known locally as a Stinker – takes off in search of another meal. On New Island, these huge birds specialise in finishing off the remains of penguins killed, but only partially eaten, by sea lions.

Walking with its family, a young Upland Goose stretches its growing wings on a Saunders Island beach. This species is common throughout the islands, and is still often hunted for its meat.

Despite their relative isolation, the Falklands lie just downwind from Cape Horn – gateway to the Pacific – a fact that nearly ensured their early discovery by mariners. Indeed, the first accepted sighting of the Falklands was in 1592 by English Captain John Davis, who, blown off course in a storm, took grateful refuge here.

However, it may not have been until a century later, in January of 1690, that the first landing was made. On that occasion the captain of the Welfare, John Strong, described stepping ashore in the islands among great flocks of penguins – many of which, almost certainly, ended up in the ship's stew pot.

Aware of the strategic position of the Falklands, the English solidified their historic claim to the islands by establishing a military post, Port Egmont, on Saunders Island, in 1765, unaware that the French had already settled in Port Louis, at the far eastern edge of the archipelago, the year before. What followed was nearly a century of intrigue and political manoeuvring, with no permanent settlement by any nation. The English abandoned Port Egmont in 1776, its garrison needed elsewhere in the world, and the French ceded Port Louis to the Spanish – who subsequently abandoned the islands.

By 1833, when Darwin landed here, the islands were in a state of near-chaos, and Port Louis, nearly destroyed two years earlier by an American gunship, was probably little more than a lawless camp. It would not be until 1842 that the British would re-assert their claim to the Falklands, and colonization begun in earnest. A year later, the main settlement was moved from Port Louis to the deep-water harbour where modern Stanley lies today. From then on, this tiny outpost of Britannia persevered, forgotten by most of the world, for the next 140 years.

A young male elephant seal tosses sand on his back to keep cool on Sea Lion Island. Only the largest bulls have a chance to breed, so this fellow has time on his hands.

With its corries and dark tarns, Mt. Usborne, the Falklands' tallest peak,
reveals the sculpting prowess of Ice Age glaciers. Even today, snow lingers
in these cold corners well into summer.

That would change abruptly in 1982, when, citing dubious claims of sovereignty (and
ignoring the simple fact that the vast majority of island residents were British - and happy
to remain so) Argentina invaded the Falklands. Calculated to distract attention from severe
economic and political problems at home, the Argentine attack prompted a swift and
decisive response from Thatcher's Britain, and despite a shocking loss of life on both sides,
the war was brief, and the islands re-taken. In the end, the war confirmed one thing
without question – that the Falklands were, and are, wholly British.

Today, a look at a map of the Falklands leaves no doubt as to the ancestry of its
inhabitants. Just look at the place names: there is a Tickle Island and a Tuppenny Rock and
a little peninsula known, inexplicably, as The Rat's Piece. There is an Anxious Passage and
a Bleaker Jump, a Smoko Mountain and a Bosom Hills. And finally, there is my favourite –
a rough sea passage in the far west, known simply as The Woolly Gut.

A pair of Ruddy-headed Geese pause for a drink at a freshwater pool on Sea Lion Island.

In ancient Europe, castles were often surrounded by "chevaux-de-frise", piles of sharpened wood designed to slow the progress of invaders – the jumbled rocks of the Falkland stone runs almost seem designed for this purpose.

History lives in these names, and with nearly every step you take in the Falklands there is history underfoot, from the stone corrals of early gauchos, to the discarded rifle shells that still litter many of the hilltops around Stanley – poignant reminders of the 1982 war.

Today, the islands are home to roughly 2500 people, more than at any other time in their history. Some are descendants of Lincolnshire farmers and Highland crofters that settled here more than a century ago. Other, more recent, arrivals have been drawn to the Falklands by the same promise that attracted the first settlers to this far edge of the world: opportunity, independence, peace - and community.

An arch of whale bones frames the spire of Christ Church Cathedral in the centre of Stanley, the main settlement in the Falklands. With its red postboxes and busy pubs, Stanley's character is unmistakably British.

Even in the heart of summer, weather in the Falklands can be both boisterous and abundant. Here an intense squall rolls over New Island, bringing heavy rain – followed by brilliant sunshine.

On Sea Lion Island, a passing summer shower douses a colony of Gentoos and leaves a rainbow in its wake. Nesting in the open air, these penguins must carry on the chores of parenthood under any conditions.

CHAPTER TWO

Coming Home

Imagine, if you can, a single moment. It is that moment, aching and irresistible, when an animal – be it penguin or petrel, seal or sea lion – intentionally turns its back on the rich shoals of fish or squid on which it has been feeding, and begins the long journey back towards a distant and invisible shore.

Every year, as spring warms the southern air, animals begin to return to the Falklands from the farthest corners of the sea, crossing thousands of miles of open water to arrive at the same crowded slab of rock or humid, dingy burrow, where they were born. It is a journey of optimism and hope – and of sacrifice. For it is a journey made, not for their own benefit, but for the sake of a generation still unborn.

Migration is an annual event in much of the animal kingdom, as much a part of life as eating or sleeping, and a fact we blithely accept without really considering how extraordinary it really is. Remember: there are no roadmaps for this journey, no landmarks to show the way, only the wind, sea and stars, and the blind pathways of genetic memory.

Long-lived and loyal, albatrosses form strong pairs, reinforced by elaborate courtship rituals. These two, however, did not seem well-suited: after a few honks and bill-claps, they wandered off in search of a better match. *New Island.*

So how does a soaring albatross find its way back across a thousand miles of open sea, to find the ledge on New Island where it nested the previous year? And how does a Rockhopper Penguin, having spent the winter feeding along the Argentine coast, know the exact route that will lead it to the rocky shores of Berkeley Sound? We have essentially no idea. (What's more, how many of us could, without nautical charts or GPS, find a rocky speck in the middle of an endless ocean?)

In recent years, scientists have used tiny transmitters to learn a great deal about where animals go, yet these costly instruments tell us nothing about how they find their way there – and back. Do they use the ever-changing stars? Are there chemical signposts in the sea that they can follow, as salmon do, to retrace their steps from childhood? The answer remains a tantalizing mystery, and one that approaches the miraculous.

For more than twenty species of seabirds, and three species of pinnipeds (literally "feather-feet" – the seals and sea lions) the Falklands provide an essential haven, close to rich feeding grounds, on which to gather and breed. With only a limited number of islands in this remote part of the world, the numbers of animals that return to the Falklands every year can be truly staggering.

On Steeple Jason, for example, a remote outlier of the main archipelago, half a million Black-browed Albatrosses breed every year, the largest single albatross colony on Earth. What's more, in the narrow gaps between the albatrosses' muddy nesting towers are crammed an additional 200,000 Rockhopper Penguins. It is, by any measure, a great city of birds: noisy, chaotic, fetid and wonderful.

Lunch is where you find it. This Tussockbird kept returning to pick flecks of discarded skin off the nose of this rather annoyed elephant seal on Sea Lion Island.

I can think of few places on the planet that compare with the raw spectacle of a seabird colony, or that display the same sheer, unadulterated exuberance of life. In every corner of this avian metropolis are endless dramas of love and loss, terror and tenderness.

In one place, two penguins squabble over a prime nest site or, perhaps, over a particularly desirable spouse. Elsewhere, a young albatross chick stretches its wings for the first time, wings that will one day allow it to circle the globe a dozen times or more.

For me, one of the greatest joys of a seabird colony is that you can sit quietly alongside this unending thrum of activity and watch, with little or no effect on the goings-on. It is a twenty-four-hour spectacle, a tireless, guano-reeking Serengeti.

Not all of the Falkland seabirds choose to nest in these dense congregations, however. In fact, the most abundant creature in the islands is one you will almost certainly never see: a tiny cousin of the albatross called the thin-billed prion. There may be as many as a million nesting pairs in the Falklands – further testimony to the abundance of food in the surrounding seas – but they are strictly nocturnal, and nest underground. In places, the nests of prions riddle the ground to the point that it is nearly impossible to take a step without crushing one of their burrows.

Wherever animals gather in such extravagant numbers, you can be sure that predators will accompany them, and the seabird colonies of the Falklands are no exception. Chief among them is the Falkland Skua, a large, fearless relative of the gull, who gets much of his food by killing other birds – or stealing their food. Skuas patrol the breeding colonies

The summer sun sets late in the evening, seen through clumps of young Tussock Grass on New Island. Summer days are deliciously long at this latitude, and the air as clear and fresh as anywhere on earth.

Two female Falkland Fur Seals squabble over a resting place, on the western shore of New Island. Soon, they will be gathered into harems of 5-10 females, under the control of breeding bulls.

of penguins and shags, eyes open for an opportunity to snatch any unguarded eggs or chicks they find. Sometimes, they are even less polite, and simply shove a parent off its nest, and take whatever they want by force.

On New Island, some skuas specialize in hunting prions, with such enthusiasm that, in places, the ground is littered with grisly reminders of their handiwork – dozens of discarded pairs of tiny grey wings, each attached to a fragile skeleton, entirely stripped of flesh. (Lest you be tempted to consider skuas nasty, unwelcome additions to the food chain, remember that their chicks are, like those of their prey, small, irresistibly fluffy, and always hungry).

Although wind is the norm in the Falklands, there are also summer days of lovely, windless calm. Here the sun brightens a quiet beach at the north end of New Island after a brief shower.

Other predators, too, are drawn to the teeming seabird colonies: among them, Kelp and Dolphin Gulls, Crested and Striated Caracaras. All take advantage of the sudden abundance of summer, when there is almost more food available than hours in the day to eat it.

One of the oddest guests at the party, however, is not a true predator, but a bold and persistent scavenger. It is the Snowy Sheathbill, a pure white bird – quite common in the icy landscape of coastal Antarctica – that subsists almost entirely on bits of spilled food and faeces. Scampering in between crowded penguin nests, the sheathbill is largely ignored: he poses no threat.

Along some remote rocky shorelines and sandy beaches of the Falklands are other annual migrants – the seals, fur seals and sea lions. First to arrive every year are the elephant seals, the largest pinnipeds in the world. A mature male elephant seal can measure six metres in length and weigh a staggering three tons or more. Bulk and power are essential because only the largest, most aggressive males will control the beaches where females will come ashore to breed in September. For the next few months, vicious battles will be fought, and dynasties toppled, in the struggle for supremacy.

Although a non-native flower, these European daisies brighten the shoreline on Bleaker Island.

A nesting pair of Rock Shags on Bleaker Island. One has just returned from a feeding trip at sea, ready to take over the responsibilities of incubating a nest full of eggs.

A pair of Falkland Fur Seals play in the crystalline water off the west side of New Island. Although once decimated by uncontrolled hunting, this species has made a striking comeback.

By the time the first snows of autumn arrive, the beaches will be largely empty of elephant seals, except for the handful still suffering through the discomforts of their annual moult. The large males, having starved themselves during the breeding season, will be gorging themselves at sea, re-building their bulk in anticipation of next year's battles. Some, especially the largest and most battle-scarred, may never return.

Most of the nesting seabirds, meanwhile, will also have left the islands, their colonies abandoned and eerily quiet. By June, they will be somewhere far out at sea, following schools of fish or teeming balls of krill until that moment – long months away - when they are once again called to land.

During a summer gale, this albatross, designed for effortless soaring, must strike a deft balance between braking and dropping, between control and chaos. It took a dozen attempts before it finally landed at its nest.

Nesting among the Tussock Grass on New Island, this Black-browed Albatross stands guard over its young chick. As the chick grows, its parents will serve as an airborne conveyor belt of squid, from sea to waiting beak.

Each nest a careful distance from its neighbours, Imperial Cormorants lay their eggs on mud-built thrones. *Rockhopper Point, Sea Lion Island.*

No more than a day old, a baby King Penguin pokes out from beneath its parent's belly. *Volunteer Point.*

A moment of tenderness between a pair of Black-browed Albatrosses on Saunders Island. The Falklands are home to two-thirds of the world's breeding birds of this species.

Murder in the afternoon. As I was sitting beside a penguin colony on Sea Lion Island, a male Upland Goose attacked and killed a Ruddy-headed Goose only a few metres away. These two species typically live side-by-side without conflict.

When a male Imperial Cormorant wants to lure a passing female to his nest site, he employs this contortionist "advertising" display. Whatever irresistible message this sends to a female is lost on me. *Sea Lion Island.*

A pair of Dolphin Gulls mate among the sea cabbage on Sea Lion Island. These small, attractive gulls are found along most of the southern coasts of Patagonia.

CHAPTER THREE

Penguin Beach

By three o'clock on a December morning, dawn is already a pale glow in the north-eastern sky. After only the briefest of summer nights, hundreds of Gentoo Penguins have begun their daily march from the breeding colony down to the sea: rush hour in the Falkland Islands.

As I sit watching from a hillside above, the penguins gather together on a beach of impossibly white sand. There they pause, waiting for others to arrive – a quorum – before they will venture into the water. To penguins, there is safety in numbers, and just beyond the breakers death may be waiting. For days, I have watched a bull sea lion patrolling this beach, picking off careless penguins in the chaos of the surf. The shoreline is littered with their carcasses.

All at once, the penguins make their move, and a hundred or more birds plunge into the water en masse. In seconds, they re-appear, leaping out of the water beyond the breaking waves, in an expression of their terror, their joy and relief. They have made it, one more time.

Ironically, penguins – so perfectly adapted for the sea – are often reluctant to go into the water. They know all too well that every day, two or three birds will not make it home again. *New Island.*

Most of us imagine penguins to be polar creatures, much more at home in a world of ice and snow than on the sandy beaches and sheep paddocks of the Falklands. Yet this is one of the world's great penguin capitals: as many as a million penguins nest in the Falklands every summer, representing five of the world's seventeen species - King, Gentoo, Rockhopper, Magellanic and Macaroni. What's more, for two of those species, the Gentoo and the Rockhopper, the Falklands are home to the largest populations on Earth.

Whatever the species, there is no mistaking a penguin. All share the unique upright stance, the rigid flippers, and some variation of that trademark waddle. And all seem inordinately fond of making noise. Penguins, it turns out, are not quiet creatures. Gather them together by the thousands and they can be deafening - perhaps the loudest, most persistent, chorus in the animal kingdom.

A pair of Falkland Skuas tear apart a baby Gentoo Penguin they have just snatched from its nest on Saunders Island. Skuas maintain feeding territories and defend them against other birds.

One evening on West Point Island, I lay down in some rather unspeakable muck to capture this eye-level portrait of penguins on the march through a tussock forest.

There are, of course, practical reasons for all this noise-making. Penguins use their voices to express their pleasure, their discontent, and their willingness to breed. And, in a colony of a thousand or more birds, a familiar voice can lead a returning penguin back to it's nest, and it's hungry chick.

I suppose everyone has a favourite penguin, and I am no exception: I have an unapologetic weakness for Rockhoppers. There is something about these scrappy, pint-sized birds that I find simply irresistible. Most of all, I admire their toughness, their apparent indifference to the worst that nature can dish out. Consider this: although there may be hundreds of low-lying shorelines in the Falklands, Rockhoppers, for reasons that strain logic, prefer nesting at the top of the highest, most inaccessible cliffs. These they climb, every day, in any weather, with a dogged persistence that borders on masochism.

On Sea Lion Island, for example, there is a near-vertical cliff that rises from the angry surf to a colony on a plateau high above. To reach it, the penguins must endure being pounded repeatedly against the rocks by the endless waves, just to gain a foothold.

Then, without any hesitation, they must start hopping up the cliff, one tiny ledge at a time, before the next wave plucks them off and drags them back down to the sea – only to begin the process again. During one particularly violent storm, with waves of terrifying size, I watched a group of "rockies" go at this for hours on end, never getting more than a few metres above the water before being snatched by another wave. Just an average day in the life of a Rockhopper.

Having dislodged a Gentoo egg from its nest, this Johnny Rook set out to break it open with his foot. It took twenty minutes to make a crack - at which point it was promptly stolen by another bird. *New Island.*

For Magellanic Penguins, by contrast, coming to land is a comparatively benign affair: they simply step out of the water and waddle ashore. And, unlike Rockhoppers, which breed in large noisy colonies, open to the elements, Magellanics prefer the privacy of a burrow, the only Falkland penguin to breed underground. This is most likely a trait inherited from their cousins on the Patagonian coast, where living in burrows is an essential defence from the intense sun and wind, and a host of predators.

The largest of the Falkland penguins, and arguably the most beautiful, is the King, aptly named for its handsome silver cape and yes, its regal bearing. Kings seem always poised and elegant, even a bit aloof. More truly Antarctic birds, Kings are vastly more abundant on islands further south than at this latitude. Indeed, the little colony at Volunteers is the northernmost major gathering of these birds in the world, and typically numbers no more than about 200-300 pairs. (By contrast, a single colony of Kings on South Georgia Island, 1000 kilometres to the southeast, may have closer to 250,000.)

Whatever their numbers, penguins need other penguins to breed, not only in the most obvious way, but also because they need the stimulus provided by being surrounded by others of their kind: the more the merrier. Without a crowd, it seems to be hard for them to get in the mood.

Sometimes they are forced to improvise. Every year, one or two King Penguins come ashore at isolated locations around the Falklands, anxious to breed, perhaps, but with no other Kings in sight. Instead, a lonely King may wander into a colony of Gentoos, apparently preferring the jostling company of these much-smaller birds to solitude. Among penguins, sociability often outweighs reason.

Watching penguins underwater is always a revelation. Never again will you pity a penguin for its flightlessness, having seen how graceful and utterly at home they are in the sea. *New Island.*

Oddly, although highly social birds, penguins don't seem to like each other very much. Look at any penguin colony, and one thing is inescapable: they like to keep their distance. They may seem impossibly packed together, but there is, in fact, always a distinct space between them. Nor is this gap of random size. It is precisely the pecking reach of an angry penguin's beak.

And they are angry a lot. Witness what happens when a penguin, be it King, Gentoo or Rockhopper, tries to get to its nest site in the middle of the colony. While nesting in the centre of a mass of birds may add some measure of safety from predators, it also means running a gauntlet of jabbing beaks every time you want to go anywhere.

(Sometimes this anti-social streak can take a more serious turn. I recently watched an adult King Penguin impale its neighbour's newly-hatched chick, killing it, in what could only be interpreted as an act of supremely bad community relations.)

After a long feeding trip at sea, the first thing a King Penguin wants to do when it gets home is take a good, long nap. These two birds spent most of the afternoon rocking on their heels, dreaming, perhaps, of great shoals of squid. *Volunteer Point.*

Every morning, Magellanic Penguins announce themselves to the world, in the loud, braying voice that earns them the name "Jackasses". This pair nested directly under our cabin on New Island and serenaded our breakfast.

By late afternoon, many of the Falkland penguins have begun to return from their feeding trips at sea. As evening comes, I climb out to the end of the Devil's Nose, a thin blade of stone that juts out from the sheer cliffs of West Point Island. Below me, I can see large rafts of Rockhoppers already forming offshore, waiting. It may take half an hour or more for them to convince themselves that no predators are lurking near the shore, so they simply swim back and forth, working up the courage to land.

Then, as if on cue, the whole group will suddenly turn and begin a mad race towards land, in a frenzied effort to be the first out of the water. At the last second they disappear, diving deeply to gain more speed, and then, suddenly, breathtakingly, begin popping out of the sea like a hundred feathered missiles. Home again.

A Dolphin Gull happily walks away with a prize, a Gentoo Penguin egg. Typically, these small gulls are not so ambitious, scavenging bits of spilled food and faeces. *Bleaker Island.*

From feathered laundry bag to elegant royalty: this young King Penguin endures the awkward transition into its first adult plumage. After a year on the colony, it will soon have to face the rigors of independence. *Volunteer Point.*

On Sea Lion Island, this coastal freshwater pond is a favourite gathering
place for Magellanic Penguins which nest in the surrounding tussock.
They come here to bathe, and, one imagines, to catch up on the news.

Rockhoppers often establish their breeding colonies along fresh water streams. Here, on Saunders Island, a bird sips at a dripping spring, unaware, or perhaps indifferent, to the fact that hundreds of other birds are nesting just upstream.

Being a penguin – especially in the squalor of a breeding colony - can be a dirty business. No surprise, then, that this Rockhopper on Saunders Island seemed grateful for a good wash.

CHAPTER FOUR

Johnny Rooks & Steamer Ducks

Simply said, the Johnny Rook is a thief and a villain – and the most fascinating creature in the Falkland Islands. Anywhere there are Johnny Rooks, nothing is safe: sandwiches are snatched, backpacks rifled and shoes stolen. Lie down for a nap and you may wake with a half dozen of them around you – apparently still debating whether you'd make a decent meal.

Most closely related to falcons, Johnny Rooks (also known as Striated Caracaras) have traded the falcon's aerial prowess for life as ground-based predators and scavengers. They feed on seabirds, eggs and chicks, and just about anything else they can sink their talons into. More than anything else, rooks are survivors – quick, cunning and resourceful.

Sometimes this resourcefulness can be painful to watch. On New Island, we discovered a pair of rooks that had fashioned a rather macabre feeding strategy, one we dubbed "chick-farming". For several days, the birds stalked the edges of the Gentoo colony below our cabin, systematically plucking out the eyes of unguarded chicks.

One learns quickly, in caracara country, not to set anything down.
Turn away and within seconds the rook will have it, and be quite
reluctant to give it back. *Sea Lion Island.*

As a cluster of young Steamer Ducks take an afternoon's rest, their parents, aggressively protective, are always close by. *Sea Lion Island.*

You don't want to tangle with an angry Steamer Duck. On Sea Lion Island, this protective father makes clear he wants me to back away: I happily complied.

This puzzled us, since they made no further attempt to capture or eat the hapless chicks – at first. Only days later did we begin to see their plan: the suppurating wounds they had inflicted would invariably invite infection. Eventually the wounded birds would weaken and die and, in a week's time, the patient rooks would simply return to collect their reward.

Not surprisingly, Johnny Rooks have few friends. Although abundant all through the islands in Darwin's day, they were considered pests by early settlers, and blamed for attacks on livestock (and, presumably, for anything that went missing, from pocket knives to socks). In 1908 a bounty was put on their heads, and their numbers plummeted. Today, they are protected by law, yet remain slow to recover: there may only be 500 pairs, largely restricted to the offshore seabird islands.

Caracaras are not only found in the Falklands: other populations exist on several islands off Cape Horn and the Chilean coast. Yet it is quite possible that the Falkland population of these birds may one day develop into a species all its own. This is the nature of islands, after all.

Isolation makes islands the playgrounds of evolution, where nature is suddenly free to re-invent herself in new and unexpected ways. Plants and animals that find themselves castaways on these remote shores can, over millennia, begin to follow different genetic paths from their mainland cousins. This process, so stunningly demonstrated among the islands of the Galapagos and Hawaii, is also at work today in the Falkland Islands.

Here, on New Island, a trio of Johnny Rooks calls together in what may be an expression of dominance, competition, or challenge. Johnny Rooks are intensely social, an uncommon trait in predators.

A bull elephant seal is many times the female's size, so when the urge strikes him, he does pretty much what he wants. This reluctant partner tried to escape into the surf, but did not get far. *Sea Lion Island.*

So far, the number of animal species that are endemic (restricted to the Falklands) remains relatively small, presumably because the islands lie so close to the Patagonian mainland. What's more, the vast majority of birds in the Falklands are seabirds, which are long-lived and travel great distances every year. Most of these are found elsewhere, and undoubtedly interbreeding between populations occurs frequently.

On the other hand, the Falklands have a number of smaller, more sedentary birds, some of which may already be drifting towards uniqueness. Among these are several that are already considered unique races or sub-species, including a thrush, a finch and a flycatcher.

Although nocturnal elsewhere, the Black-crowned Night-heron has no competition on the Falklands, and feeds in the daytime as well. This one hunts along the edge of a freshwater pond on Sea Lion Island.

There is, however, one bird that is already unique – the Falkland Flightless Steamer Duck. Though related to a similar bird in South America, this species has lived long enough on this far-flung archipelago to become quite distinct. As their name would suggest, Steamers have lost their ability to fly, and rely on rough paddling to get around. Clearly, relinquishing the ability to fly comes at a price – just ask a penguin at the bottom of a cliff – but Falkland Steamers seem to have made the most of it. They are big (a full-grown male may weigh over 4 kilograms) and aggressive, and so have little to fear from predators like the skua or Johnny Rook.

They also needn't travel far to get their food. In fact, a pair of Steamer Ducks may live their entire lives along a single rocky shoreline, feeding on shellfish and invertebrates. With no need for escape, and with food literally at their doorstep, flight has become largely irrelevant.

Until recently, the Steamer was considered the Falkland's only truly endemic bird. But recently, a new one has been added to the list: the little Cobb's Wren. Once considered just a form of the southern House Wren, common throughout South America, it is now a full-fledged species on its own. Congratulations are in order.

Although birds have perhaps been slow to evolve new forms in the Falklands over the millennia, plants have been relatively busy. Because they are sessile and their populations easily isolated, plants seem to evolve with relative ease. As a result, the Falklands can boast of a variety of endemic plants. One of the most striking of these is Nassauvia serpentia, commonly known as the Snake Plant.

Patrolling the kelp beds along the shores of Sea Lion Island, this Blackish Oystercatcher feeds on shellfish and small invertebrates.

Two young elephant seals practice their fighting skills along the beach on Sea Lion Island. It may be ten years or more before they will have a chance to breed, when this playful sparring turns deadly serious.

This rather bizarre composite grows only within the jumbled rocks of the Falkland stone runs – and nowhere else on earth. Its stems may reach two metres in length, long enough to reach up through the burden of stones to the light. Rare, exotic, uniquely specialized: one expects oddballs like this to be difficult to find, yet you can usually find Nassauvia serpentia within a few minutes on any of the major stone runs just west of Stanley.

Most of the Falkland's other endemics are, by comparison, small and inconspicuous, the sort of things you would expect in a windy, treeless landscape such as this. One of them, Nassauvia gaudichaudii, is a close relative of the Snake Plant, yet it is almost unrecognisable as such, growing in moss-like cushions, close to the ground. (It is quite possible, of course, that Nassauvia serpentia itself once grew this way as well, but co-evolved with the stone runs as they were formed. Buried under a river of moving stones, they may have been forced to find their way up to the light, resulting in the long twisting snake plants of today. It is an intriguing thought.)

Besides the Snake Plant, the most showy, and most unexpected, of the endemic plants in the Falklands is one that also very nearly vanished: the Felton's Flower. This is a stunning bloom of deep, velvety magenta, with bright yellow stamens. Thought to be extinct in the wild as recently as 1997, Felton's Flower was then re-discovered in a few isolated corners, and is now being cultivated in many island gardens. The flower was named for Arthur Felton, who transplanted it into his garden on West Point Island in 1895, a place where it still thrives today. (But look when the sun is shining – for the flower only opens in full sunshine!)

Johnny Rooks defend their food vigorously: this one is marching over to threaten an interloper. The bird's menacing posture and intense stare makes clear his message – clear off!

Although the Falklands have been continuously inhabited for nearly two centuries, and in many areas, heavily altered by human activity, much of the archipelago is still largely wild. As a result, there are almost certainly new plants yet to be discovered in some remote valleys or offshore islands. Insects, too, have not been well-studied in the Falklands, and there may be a number of new species awaiting discovery. And there is always the chance that the next gust of wind from Patagonia will bring a new visitor: a butterfly, a seed, or perhaps, a lost and desperate bird. In either case, a pioneer.

Few plants have evolved in such a specialised habitat as the Snake Plant.
Unique to the Falklands, it grows only within the rocky recesses of the
stone runs.

The rugged western coast of New Island on
a late summer evening. Strong winds keep
the islands bare of trees. Tussock Grass,
however, plays a similar ecological role.

Falkland plants tend to be low-growing, with inconspicuous flowers. This Prickly-burr (Acaena magellanica) is a common resident of open areas near the sea. *Carcass Island.*

A Falkland Thrush rests on a fallen branch on Carcass Island. Carcass has been kept free of rats and, as a result, has an abundance of small birds.

This Gaudichaudi's Orchid is named for French botanist, Charles Gaudichaud-Beaupre (1789 - 1854), who was shipwrecked in the Falklands in 1820 aboard the expedition ship Uranie.

CHAPTER FIVE

Currents of Change

The route was steep and rough, the wind fierce. Stepping carefully from boulder to boulder, we climbed slowly, struggling to stay upright as gusts of wind threatened to blow us off our feet. Eventually, the grade eased and we emerged onto the barren crest of Mt. Usborne. Doffing our packs with relief, we rested at the foot of the summit cairn, enjoyed a warming cup of tea, and looked out over a spectacular, nearly endless, view.

Seen from this highest point in the islands, the Falkland landscape appears largely untouched. There are no roads or houses visible, no wandering fence lines, just miles of rocky hills and undulating plains, as far as the eye can see. It appears, in fact, very much as it did a thousand years ago.

Yet this vision of untouched wilderness is deceptive. For in the four hundred years since their discovery, the Falklands have been significantly altered by the hand of man. At first, the change was slow, as the absence of large-scale agriculture kept the land largely untilled and left much of the archipelago in a relatively wild state.

A stand of tussock re-asserts itself at the north end of New Island. Decimated by browsing sheep, tussock is often slow to return without hand-planting and protective fencing.

Things changed dramatically, however, in the 19th century with the advent of permanent settlement and the large-scale importation of livestock. As many as 80,000 head of cattle were being tended on East Falkland in the 1840's, when Darwin landed here, to be followed by the hundreds of thousands of sheep that are tended in the islands today.

The release of thousands of grazing animals onto the landscape has had a dramatic impact on what was once a pristine, sub-Antarctic eco-system. It brought special ruin to native plants: from tiny flowers to giant Tussock Grass – the Falkland equivalent of a forest - many natives have vanished entirely from large areas of the islands, largely because of grazing and the introduction of aggressive, non-native plants such as gorse.

To make matters worse, ships and sailors introduced animals such as rats and feral cats, which have had a devastating effect on many of the islands' native animals, especially small birds, the vast majority of which evolved with no land-based predators. The contrast is striking: on rat-free islands, the air is filled with the songs of siskins and finches. Where rats exist, there is only silence.

And although it is easy to think of the Falklands as a wildlife paradise, it is a paradise populated by ghosts. The mid-19th century was a true holocaust for the seabirds and marine mammals in these islands. At the height of the sealing and whaling industries in the southern oceans, wildlife often grimly shared a common, fate: being clubbed to death for their skins, flensed for their meat or simply boiled up to produce oil. At times, the pace of this slaughter was breathtaking. elephant seals,

The first thing most penguins do when they come out of the water is to settle in for a good scratch, a task made more challenging by the fact that they have neither hands nor knees.

As penguin chicks get bigger, they get more active – and more annoying. No longer content to sit on the nest and wait to be fed, they often chase their parents through the colony. *Sea Lion Island.*

for example, were driven almost to extinction in the Falklands by 1860, and fur seals were reduced to such small numbers that no one bothered hunting them anymore. And when the seals were gone, the hunters turned to penguins.

In 1867 one ship is said to have collected more than 50,000 gallons of penguin oil from the Falkland Islands, a sum which required the killing of nearly 500,000 birds in that season alone. (By this grisly equation, a rendered penguin was only good for about one and a half cups of oil.)

With this scale of depredation, it is hard to imagine how any wildlife survived here at all. Yet once the hunting was eventually outlawed, or simply abandoned for lack of

These Rockhopper Penguins seem to prefer the quiet of the tussock to the chaos of the main colony on New Island. To reach their nests, they must follow dark tunnels under the overhanging vegetation.

profits, the animal populations gradually rebounded, a testimony to the enormous productivity of the surrounding oceans.

Today, however, changes in that same ocean may spell trouble for the future of wildlife in the Falklands. Consider the Rockhopper penguin: in the 1930's the Falkland population of this species was believed to have been about one million pairs. But subsequent census data revealed a dramatic decrease in their numbers; a survey in 1995/6 counted only 263,000 pairs, a drop of roughly 75%.

Is this, as some have claimed, a direct result of competition with commercial fisheries? Or is it an artifact of Global Warming, with its accompanying changes in sea temperature and food availability. Or are animal populations naturally dynamic, simply fluctuating on cycles we can neither see nor understand? You can easily find articulate advocates for each of these positions, but the truth is consistently, maddeningly, elusive.

This is often the case, for the sea can be a dark and mysterious place, revealing its secrets only with great reluctance. Occasionally, we can witness dramatic events in the marine eco-system, monitor them closely, and still not understand what is going on. I was in the Falklands in December of 2002, for example, and witnessed a catastrophic die-off of seabirds in the western islands. Many of us watched, in horror, as thousands of adult Gentoo Penguins suddenly began to weaken and die at the height of the season.

Sheep-rearing and wildlife are surprisingly compatible, a fact which has allowed penguins and other seabirds to persist here, despite the widespread human impact on the islands. *Saunders Island.*

They were not starving: when food is scarce adults simply abandon their chicks and try again the following year. In this case, however, the birds were struck by some sort of neurological disease that caused them to lose motor control, and ultimately collapse. (Predators like Johnny Rooks had, as you can imagine, a field day.)

Preliminary evidence seemed to point to a massive red tide event, perhaps brought on by warmer-than-normal sea temperatures. But subsequent autopsies were ambiguous, and no final explanation was agreed upon. Again was this a purely natural event, or a sign of environmental changes caused by human activity? We don't know, but whatever the cause, it may take years for some of the affected colonies to recover.

At other times, however, our impact on the marine environment is well-documented – and catastrophic. One such case is the massive loss of albatross caught every year in long-lines and fishing nets off the Falklands. Although there is accidental mortality, or "by-catch", in any commercial fishing operation, the deaths of literally thousands of birds every season threatens the entire population.

In these cases, it is essential to either change the fishing technique to avoid this massive by-catch, or stop the fishing altogether. New fishing guidelines are already being developed in the Falklands to end this devastating slaughter.

A young albatross waits patiently for its parents to return with food. With nothing else to do for days at a time, simply watching a photographer is a diversion. *West Point Island.*

Rock and surf on New Island. This island, in the far west, is divided into two private nature reserves, each with a separate owner, but a shared mission to see the wildlife protected.

Evening light shines in the ruby-coloured eye of a Rockhopper Penguin on Bleaker Island. The world's largest population of Rockies lives in the Falklands, making this a vital refuge for the species.

During the early summer of 2002/3, thousands of Gentoo Penguins
suddenly began to die, and squads of hungry Johnny Rooks made short
work of the many carcasses. *New Island.*

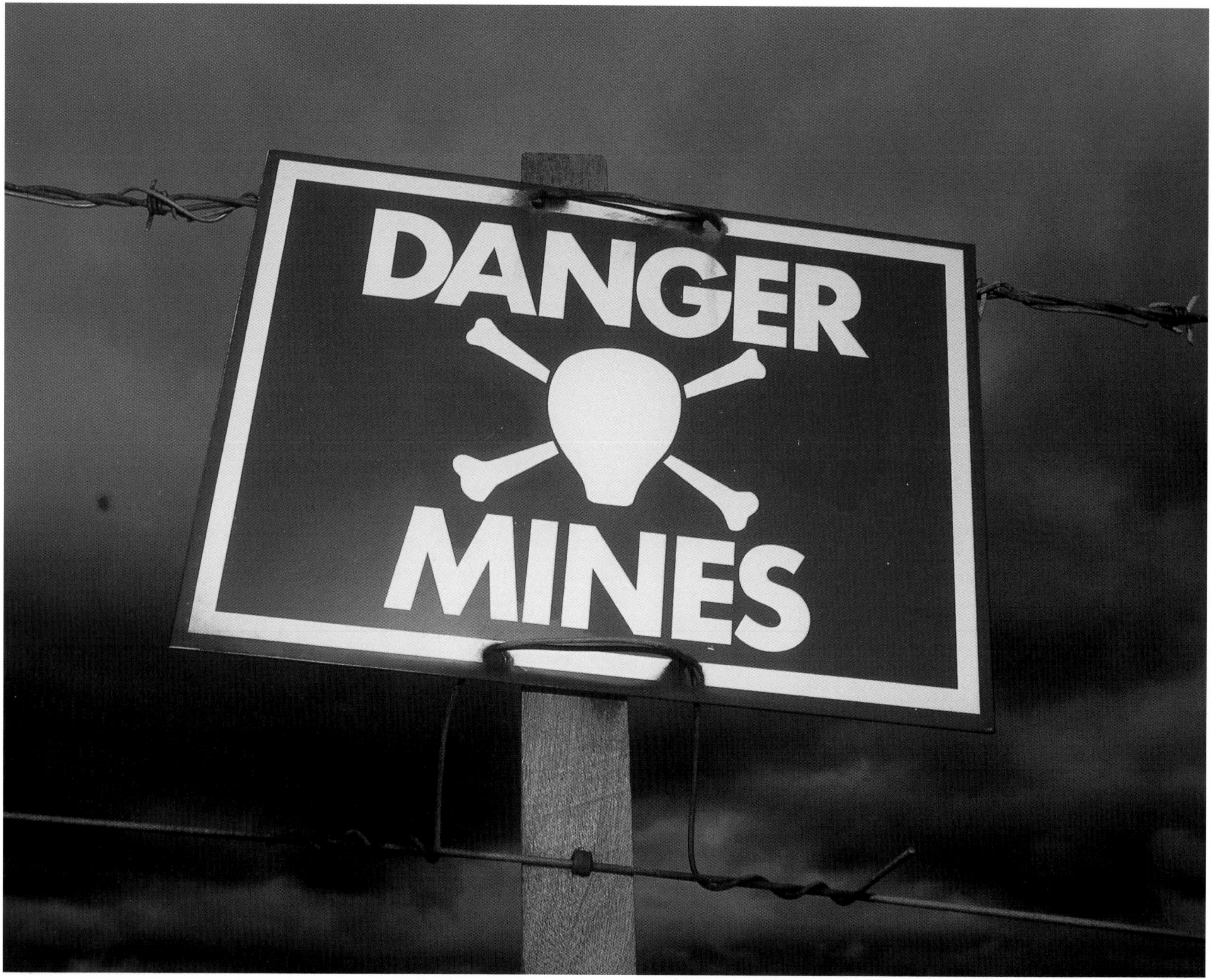
DANGER
MINES

Many areas of East Falkland were mined during the 1982 conflict, and cannot be safely cleared. Scattered across the landscape, these signs serve as a grim reminder of the legacy of war.

Killer Whales are common in the Falklands, where they specialise in hunting seals and sea lions – and the occasional penguin. Here on Sea Lion Island, an affection for whales is given bold expression.

My wife Marty sketches Rockhoppers on Saunders Island. Tourism is growing rapidly in the Falklands, which brings both new opportunities and new challenges.

The news for Falkland wildlife, meanwhile, is not unrelievedly grim. There is a new ecological awareness at work in the islands, and a greater appreciation for the natural treasures that they possess. Many wildlife reserves have been created, both public and private, to protect some of the most important animal and plant communities in the Falklands.

Meanwhile, tourism in the Falklands - nearly unheard of only a decade ago - is booming. More than 27,000 visitors arrived in the islands by cruise ship during one recent summer season, bringing considerable income to the islands. This influx of tourists may incur some negative impact, but it also provides additional incentive to protect the islands' wildlife resources, which the vast majority of these visitors have come to see.

The master of Carcass Island, Rob McGill. In recent years, some landowners, like Rob, have turned to wildlife tourism to supplement – or even replace – their income from farming.

There is, inevitably, change ahead for the Falklands. Fishing, tourism, oil development, global warming: all bring challenges that affect both human and animal residents of these islands. The greatest challenge will be to make the choices necessary to adapt to these changes, without threatening the things that make these unique, magical islands so extraordinary.

Photo Notes

It should come as no surprise that the greatest challenge to photography in the Falklands is not the animals, but the weather. I hate to think how many times the wind has blown over my tripod, or coated my lens with driving mist. Or, more often, when simply venturing outdoors seemed both uncomfortable and unprofitable.

Yet, whatever difficulties the climate throws your way, wildlife photography in the Falklands is among the most satisfying in the world. I have found that, if approached slowly and with respect, penguins and other Falkland animals tend to go about their business with no particular interest in my presence. For this reason, it is possible to be a passive witness to all the life-and-death drama that is so much a part of colonial life: murder, romance and tenderness – all take place a thousand times a day .

For the record, all of the images in this book were made with Nikon cameras, and nearly all shot on Fuji transparency film , chosen for its brilliant colour and fine grain. I always carry a tripod, not just to support long lenses – hardly necessary in the Falklands – but to hold the camera steady in the wind and weather.

Meanwhile, as I write this, the digital world is dawning, and I have made a few tentative steps across this brave frontier: in fact, a handful of the images I've included were made with a Nikon D100 digital camera.

Sadly, one of the side-effects of the digital revolution is a gradual erosion in our confidence that photographs represent real events. At one time, photography's greatest gift was its authenticity, but today it is too easy to create pictures entirely within the computer, or to alter existing ones to suit the whim – or the conscience – of the photographer. The result? Any delight we may feel at seeing a picture of unique animal behaviour, or a moment of brilliant, fleeting light, is slowly being replaced by a vague sense of suspicion. In my view, that is a tragedy.

For this reason, I feel that it is important for me to stress that all of the pictures I've included in this book are of real events, un-staged, un-manipulated and fundamentally unaltered in any way, other than the obvious biases of film, lens, light and vision.

Kevin Schafer
October 2003

A Johnny Rook looks about ready to snap a picture but he had other things in mind: namely, eating the camera. A case lesson in keeping an eye on your gear when caracaras are about.

A male Kelp Goose wanders across the thick
beds of Durvillaea kelp along the shore of
Sea Lion Island.

The Falkland Islands

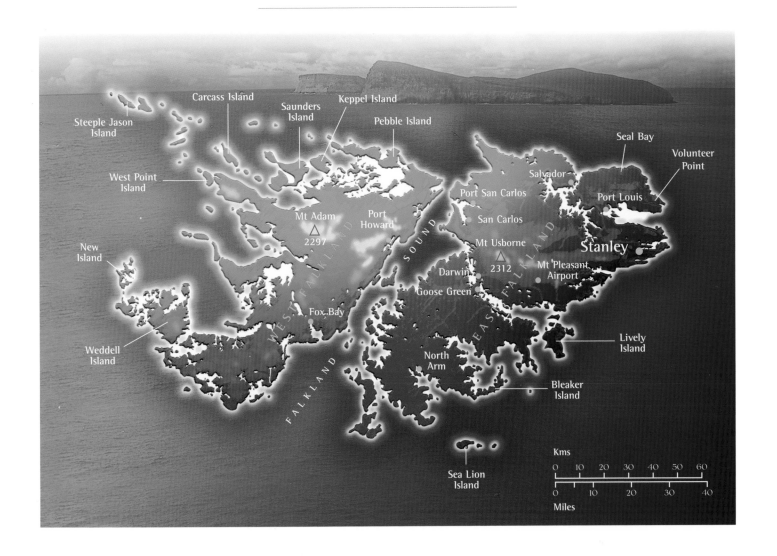

Steeple Jason Island

Carcass Island

Saunders Island

Keppel Island

Pebble Island

Seal Bay

Volunteer Point

West Point Island

Salvador

Port San Carlos

Port Louis

New Island

San Carlos

Mt Adam
△
2297

Port Howard

Mt Usborne
△
2312

Stanley

Darwin

Mt Pleasant Airport

Goose Green

Weddell Island

Fox Bay

SOUND

WEST FALKLAND

EAST FALKLAND

Lively Island

North Arm

FALKLAND

Bleaker Island

Sea Lion Island

Kms

| 0 | 10 | 20 | 30 | 40 | 50 | 60 |

| 0 | 10 | 20 | 30 | 40 |

Miles

Bibliography & Links

Barnard, Charles H.
(ed. Dodge)

Marooned
(Wesleyan Univ. Press, 1979)

Marooned on Falklands for a year in 1813, this personal drama gives some insight into the islands' early days.

Darwin, Charles

The Voyage of the Beagle
(Modern Library, 2001)

Darwin only briefly mentions the Falklands, and not with any great enthusiasm.

Pettingill, Eleanor

Penguin Summer
(Clarkson N. Potter, 1960)

A delightful story of time spent in the Falklands, with glimpses of island life as it was a half-century ago.

Pettingill, Olin Sewall

Another Penguin Summer
(Charles Scribner's Sons, 1975)

My first look at the Falklands. This follow-up volume to Penguin Summer, this includes his black-and-white photographs of the Falklands wildlife.

Schafer, Kevin

Penguin Planet
(NorthWord Press, 2001)

My tribute to these most popular of birds.

Chater, Tony

The Falklands
(Penna Press, 1996)

A delightful book, by a talented photographer and artist, filled with natural and human history, as well as personal stories of life in the islands, many of them hilarious.

Strange, Ian

The Falkland Islands and their Natural History,
(David and Charles, 1987)

The best available general book on natural subjects in the Falklands.

Strange, Ian

A Field Guide to the Wildlife of the Falkland Islands
(HarperCollins, 1992)

An essential companion in the field for identification of birds and mammals in the Falklands. Some selected plants as well.

Summers, Debbie   **A Visitor's Guide to the Falkland Islands**
(Falklands Conservation, 2001)

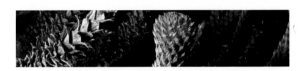

Designed primarily for cruise ship visitors, this small volume has good maps and information for some of the most popular spots in the Falklands.

Woods, Robin   **Flowering Plants of the Falkland Islands**
(Falklands Conservation, 2000)

A handy field guide to the most common, and interesting, plants in the Falklands.

Links

Falklands Conservation: **www.falklandsconservation.com**

This important organisation is devoted to preserving the natural treasures of these magical islands. Become a member!

Falklands Tourist Board: **www.tourism.org.fk.**

For practical information on visiting the islands, either through a tour, or independently.

An outcrop of rock along the shoreline of Caracuss Island is covered with brilliant yellow lichens.